ESSAYS IN INTERNATIONAL FINANCE

No. 163, July 1986

GERMAN REPARATIONS AND BRAZILIAN DEBT: A COMPARATIVE STUDY

ARMINIO FRAGA

INTERNATIONAL FINANCE SECTION

DEPARTMENT OF ECONOMICS
PRINCETON UNIVERSITY
PRINCETON, NEW JERSEY

Library of Congress Cataloging-in-Publication Data

Fraga, Arminio
German reparations and Brazilian debt.

(Essays in international finance, ISSN 0081-142X; no. 163) (July 1986))
Bibliography: p.
1. Debts, External—Brazil. 2. Petroleum products—Prices. 3. Debts, External—Germany. 4. World War, 1914-1918—Reparations. I. Title. II. Series: Essays in international finance; no. 163.
HJ8579.F7 1986   336.3′4′0943   86-15386
ISBN 0-88165-070-6 (pbk.)

Printed in the United States of America by Princeton University Press at Princeton, New Jersey.

International Standard Serial Number: 0071-142X
International Standard Book Number: 0-88165-070-6
Library of Congress Catalog Card Number: 86-15386

CONTENTS

GERMAN REPARATIONS AND BRAZILIAN DEBT: A COMPARATIVE STUDY

> The net results of the process . . . have been: (1) a constant increase, rather than decrease, of international indebtedness; (2) a steady growth in the volume of annual foreign payments to be made by this country and the other net debtor countries; and (3) a continuous disguising of the difficulties inherent in the situation by new international loans.
>
> Moulton and Pasvolsky (1932, p. 301).

1 Introduction

Although the passage quoted above was written in 1932 about Germany and the interwar debt problem, it seems to apply just as well to the current Brazilian situation. In 1931, U.S. President Herbert Hoover declared a moratorium on war debts and reparations, including almost all German payments. At the end of 1982, when Germany would still have been paying reparations, Brazil was rescued from a balance-of-payments crisis by a package that once again included the U.S. government, this time together with the International Monetary Fund, private banks, and other institutions. This essay compares the two crises, seemingly different in origin and separated by fifty-one years, and shows that they teach the same basic lesson.

I have chosen to approach this problem using the method of historical economics, the term Kindleberger (1978, p. 7) uses to distinguish it from conventional economic history. Historical economics is concerned with the analysis of economic processes and structures rather than the pursuit of new factual detail. I examine the two debt crises in the light of old and new theories of balance-of-payments adjustment, and of theories of optimal borrowing. Instead of performing formal statistical tests, I discuss each case closely. While such an exercise in small-sample analysis necessarily calls for many judgments and qualifiers, allowing much room for "dangerous" rhetorical argument, I hope that readers will find the comparison fruitful and the conclusions persuasive. I hope, too, that some will be challenged to apply the approach to other cases.

Sections 2 and 3 briefly review the German and Brazilian experiences, focusing mainly on the interaction of external shocks, domestic policies, and foreign lending. Section 4 compares the impact on Germany of the payment of reparations with the impact on Brazil of higher oil prices. Section 5 looks

This essay is a revised version of the third chapter of my dissertation. I am grateful to William Branson, my thesis supervisor, and a referee.

critically at the behavior of countries as borrowers and of banks as lenders. The last section draws the basic lesson for borrowers and lenders.

2 A Review of the German Experience, 1919-31[1]

The end of World War I marked the beginning of one of the most complex periods in German history, running from the Treaty of Versailles to the Nazi seizure of power. Germany provided the stage for events rich in opportunities for scholarly research of every sort. In the economic sphere, reparations, budget deficits, and other developments led to large internal and external imbalances. What follows is a brief review of the main economic events of the Weimar period, focusing primarily on the relationship between external and domestic developments.

The Treaty of Versailles, signed on June 28, 1919, sealed the destiny of Germany for some time. It was required to pay for a large share of the war burden, though an exact amount was not specified at that time; as Angell (1932, p. 11) put it, a "vast blank check" was signed. A Reparations Commission was created to study the problem, and it took almost two years to determine the size of the payment. In the interim, the issue was debated heatedly. In a famous speech, Sir Eric Geddes supported the extraction of a large indemnity: "I have personally no doubt we will get everything out of her that you can squeeze out of a lemon and a bit more" (quoted in Mayer, 1967, p. 157). Keynes was the main figure on the other side. Having dropped out of the British delegation at Versailles when he decided that events were moving toward disaster, he quickly wrote *The Economic Consequences of the Peace*, which argued forcefully that the reparations payments discussed initially at Versailles were far too high and that the peace was to be Carthaginian. He accused Clemenceau of trying to "weaken and destroy Germany in every possible way" (1919, p. 150). Postwar prosperity, he argued, would require not only a lower level of reparations but also a cancellation of inter-Ally indebtedness incurred during the war (p. 270).

The final figure of 132 billion gold marks (more than two years' GNP at that point) was reached in April 1921 and adopted officially at the London conference in early May. The "London Schedule of Payments" called for annual payments of 2 billion gold marks plus 26 percent of the value of Germany's exports. This second requirement provided some flexibility by tying payments to revenues, but it was not flexible enough. After numerous delays in German payments, the Reparations Commission agreed on August 31, 1922, to a six-month moratorium on all German obligations. But before it had ex-

[1] The main sources for the discussion that follows are Moulton and Pasvolsky (1932), *The Economist* (1932), Aldcroft (1977), Angell (1932), and Harris (1935).

pired, and despite British opposition, for political reasons Germany was declared to be in default. French and Belgian troops marched into the Ruhr in January 1923.

The following months rank among the most intensively studied periods in economics literature. Germany responded to the invasion by a sort of fiscal passive resistance. The invasion took away many revenue sources, but the Weimar government did not raise other taxes. Furthermore, expenditures on subsidies and unemployment compensation rose, so Germany ran very large fiscal deficits. The stage was set for the hyperinflation and depreciation of the mark that have been the subject of many studies. This is not the place to join the controversy over whether the inflation and deflation were caused primarily by the budget deficit or by the balance-of-payments problem. It suffices for my purposes to quote from W. Arthur Lewis (1949, pp. 23-24):

> A runaway inflation may derive from three sources. First it may be due to upward adjustments of wages, e.g. under trade union pressure. As wages rise, prices rise. The advantage of the increased money wage is thus largely offset, and a further wage increase is demanded. This leads to a further rise in prices, and the cycle may continue unchecked. Secondly, it may be set in motion by the depreciation of the foreign exchange value of the currency, e.g. because of an adverse balance of payments. This raises the cost of imports, and therefore the cost of living. Wages then rise, if linked to the cost of living, prices rise further, and the foreign exchange value falls still more, setting the cycle in motion. Thirdly it may be due to a budget deficit financed by increasing the amount of money in circulation. If money increases faster than the volume of goods (and this is inevitable after full employment is reached), prices rise. This makes the government need more money, the issue of which causes prices to rise still more. It also causes trade unions to press for higher wages, and the foreign exchange value of the currency to fall, each of which enforces the inflationary trend.
>
> The German inflation had some of all these elements.

It had indeed!

On October 15, 1923, a new currency, the Rentenmark, was introduced, along with fiscal reforms, and soon the inflation ended. The spectacular success of the disinflation plan has generally been credited to the fiscal reforms and their impact on the public's confidence in the new currency. A more efficient system of taxation banished the fear of budget deficits and the monetary expansion needed to accommodate them, and this change in expectations explains the relatively low cost of the stabilization.[2] Shortly thereafter, the government implemented a comprehensive plan to complete the stabilization of the German economy and revive the flow of reparations.

The Dawes Plan, made public in April 1924, was part of an effort whose "essential aim was to restore confidence in Germany and permit the rehabil-

[2] Bresciani-Turroni (1937) and, more recently, Sargent (1983) are the chief proponents of this view.

itation of her currency while at the same time securing reparation for her creditors" (*The Economist*, 1932, p. 2). The Plan recognized the need for a second moratorium on reparations and arranged for Germany to borrow 800 million Reichsmark in foreign capital markets. (The Reichsmark was the currency that came with the final reform, replacing the Rentenmark; 4.2 Reichsmarks were equivalent to 1 dollar.) The foreign-currency proceeds of this loan were to be deposited at the newly created Reichsbank to provide the necessary backing for the new currency. As Kindleberger (1984, p. 303) points out, the Dawes loan was not intended to "recycle the entirety of German reparation, as the French sought, but merely to prime the pump." As we shall see, it did elicit a substantial inflow of foreign funds.

The Plan made an explicit distinction between the collection of reparation payments within Germany and their transfer to foreign creditors.

Table 1 shows the schedule for the first step, the collection of funds to be deposited in a reparations account with the Reichsbank. The first two years were the "budget moratorium period," when no budget surplus was required. The next two years were the "transition period," when the budget was to show a surplus and other payments would also increase. The final year was the "standard year," representing the expected steady state.

The second step in the payment of reparations, the transfer to foreigners, was to be controlled by a transfer committee with the cooperation of the German authorities. Except for an agreement to be "cooperative," Germany's responsibility ended with the deposits in Reichsmark shown in Table 1. There was to be no fixed schedule for their conversion and transfer to the Allies, because it was believed that Germany's export surplus was unpredictable and

TABLE 1
THE DAWES PLAN: SCHEDULE OF SUMS TO BE RAISED WITHIN GERMANY
(in millions of RM)

	Budget Moratorium		Transition		Standard Year
Source	1924-25	1925-26	1926-27	1927-28	1928-29
Budget surplus	None	None	110	500	1,250
Transport tax [a]	None	250	290	290	290
Railroad securities [b]	200	845	550	660	660
Industrial bonds [b]	None	125	250	300	300
Total	1,000 [c]	1,220	1,200	1,750	2,500

[a] An off-budget item.

[b] Interest and amortization payments on these bonds and securities were to be earmarked for payment of reparations.

[c] Includes the Reichsmark counterpart of the Dawes loan.

SOURCE: Moulton and Pasvolsky (1932, p. 163).

that payments should be made only when conditions were favorable in the foreign-exchange market. If the amount in the domestic reparations account came to exceed RM2 billion owing to transfer difficulties, the transfer committee was to invest the excess funds in Germany. If the amount in the account topped RM5 billion, further contributions were to be reduced until the foreign-exchange situation improved. Arrangements were also made to correct for fluctuations in the price of gold and to increase payments in periods of prosperity. Following the spirit of classical transfer theory, no specific measures were contemplated to promote trade surpluses. This was never a problem, however, because capital inflows more than covered the payment of reparations and the trade deficit.

The first five years of the Dawes Plan marked a period of spectacular recovery for Germany. Industrial production more than doubled between January 1924 and March 1928, and the balance of payments was in surplus in every year except 1927 (see Table 2). There was no transfer problem; on the contrary, Germany ran trade deficits in every year except 1926. In effect, net transfers were being made *toward* Germany, as many authors have pointed out.

These net transfers were made possible by the massive capital inflows triggered by the Dawes loan. The capital flows took two main forms: long-term bonds sold to the public in many countries, but mainly in the United States, and short-term bank credits, including acceptances and cash advances (see Table 2). This injection of resources was crucial:

> Industry was short of capital, the financial markets were disorganized, the savings of countless Germans had been obliterated during the hyperinflation, [and] there was a chronic balance-of-payments [trade balance] deficit at any level of economic activity short of a depression. (Falkus, 1975, p. 452.)

A combination of tight domestic monetary policy (with some fine tuning) and a high level of demand for working capital led to high interest rates. This helps explain the inflow of capital that took place between 1924 and 1928 in spite of warnings by Keynes (1919), Moulton (1924), and others that Germany would have trouble repaying its debts and reparations. Throughout the 1924-28 period, capital flows played the important double role of providing the impetus for recovery and financing trade deficits as they arose.

By the first half of 1928, the Dawes Plan had apparently succeeded: the recovery was strong and reparations were being paid on schedule. As was shortly discovered, however, this impression was misleading in more than one respect.

First, even though the Dawes Plan transfers were being made, the internal collection of funds was lagging behind. As Table 3 shows, Germany ran budget deficits in every year between 1924 and 1930 except the first, in which it was expected to run a deficit. Furthermore, the figures for the federal def-

TABLE 2

GERMANY'S BALANCE OF PAYMENTS

(in millions of RM)

	1924	1925	1926	1927	1928	1929	1930	1931	1932	1933
Exports	7,810	9,546	10,677	11,118	12,627	113,632	12,175	9,733	5,834	4,957
Imports	−9,626	−11,990	−9,884	−14,078	−13,938	−13,676	−10,617	6,955	−4,782	−4,288
Trade balance	−1,816	−2,444	793	−2,960	−1,311	−44	1,558	2,778	1,052	669
Reparations	−281	−1,057	−1,191	−1,584	−1,990	−2,337	−1,716	−988	−160	−149
Interest payments	159	−6	−173	−345	−563	−800	−1,000	−1,200	−900	−700
Other services	274	462	532	645	672	712	538	450	265	232
Current account	−1,664	−3,045	−39	−4,244	−3,192	−2,469	−620	−1,040	257	52
Long-term loans	1,000	1,124	1,376	1,765	1,698	414	805	−85	14	−50
Short-term loans	1,506	307	147	1,717	1,425	1,011	431	772	−763	−447
Indefinable	413	1,704	−916	310	1,000	879	−746	−3,350	236	−79
Capital account	2,919	3,135	607	3,792	4,123	2,304	490	−2,693	−513	−576
Change in gold and foreign-exchange reserves	1,255	90	568	−452	931	−165	−130	−1,653	−256	−524

SOURCE: Harris (1935).

TABLE 3
ECONOMIC INDICATORS FOR GERMANY

	Industrial Production (1913–100)	Wholesale Prices (1913–100)	Real Wages [a] (1913–100)	Budget Deficit [b] (RM billion)	Gross Fixed Investment (RM billion)	National Income (RM billion)
1924	77	136	70	−0.5	n.a.	n.a.
1925	92	139	87	0.1	10.3	57
1926	87	129	90	0.8	10.7	n.a.
1927	110	135	97	0.3	13.0	n.a.
1928	113	136	108	1.2	13.8	n.a.
1929	114	131	110	0.9	12.8	71
1930	99	114	105	0.9	10.4	n.a.
1931	82	98	100	n.a.	6.5	n.a.
1932	66	86	94	n.a.	4.2	41

[a] Weekly earnings, twelve or more industries.

[b] Federal government only. Surplus = (−). Fiscal year ending in March of the following year.

SOURCE: Bry (1960, pp. 326, 327, 362), Moulton and Pasvolsky (1932, p. 281), Balderston (1983, p. 401), and Machlup (1964, p. 383).

icits underestimate the overall public-sector deficit. The German public debt, federal and local, totaled RM24.2 billion on March 31, 1931, of which 18.2 billion was contracted between 1924 and 1931 (Moulton and Pasvolsky, 1932, p. 283). We can thus safely say that the planned Dawes Plan surpluses never materialized and the classical transfer process that was supposed to implement the Plan never had a chance to operate because the budget never exerted deflationary pressure.

Real wages rose by more than 50 percent between 1924 and 1928 (see Table 3). This was a consequence of standard business-cycle factors and of the 1918 Stinnes-Legien Agreement, which increased the power of labor unions, in the social-democratic spirit of the Weimar Republic. This also interfered with the standard transfer theory, which calls for belt-tightening by way of reductions in real wages.

Prospects for the German economy were clouded by low levels of capital formation. Germany was borrowing but not investing. Some loans were obtained to provide working capital, and many were used for public amenities. As Dr. Schacht, the President of the Reichsbank, pointed out at the time,

> The expenditure upon the construction of stadia, swimming baths . . . , planetaria, aerodromes, theatres, and museums, upon credit concessions to, and participation in, private business, amounts to a total sum not much below the total foreign loans raised by the cities. (Cited by Harris, 1935, p. 2.)

Finally, Germany's foreign accounts were becoming increasingly fragile as foreign liabilities accumulated. The growth of short-term debt made the situation particularly delicate. Most of this debt took the form of interbank credits, which could be withdrawn suddenly. Some of the money obtained in this way was used appropriately to finance trade, but some was used to build up working capital and finance budget deficits:

> The German banks, their ledgers swelled with foreign balances, financed their various public and private undertakings freely with little thought for the morrow. Beguiled by a deceptive appearance of prosperity they borrowed short and lent long; for though their lending was in the form of short-term loans, the purposes to which many of the loans were devoted were not appropriate for this type of financing, and as the event proved they rapidly became "frozen." (Harris, 1935, p. 6.)

Summing up, between 1924 and 1928 Germany was able to stage an externally financed recovery. It maintained high rates of growth at the cost of increasing its vulnerability to further shocks. Already faced with the need to pay reparations and repay a growing debt, Germany would also have to deal with higher wages, budget deficits, and a large volume of short-term foreign liabilities. Although all reparations payments were made on schedule up to 1929, the standard year of the Dawes Plan, there was talk about new reparations arrangements as early as June 1928 (Kindleberger, 1984, p. 304). Economic activity had begun to show signs of cooling in mid-1927, and the turning point came in the summer of 1928:

> From July 1928 the flow of foreign capital, even at higher interest rates, dropped markedly. By the early autumn the Disconto-Gesellschaft was attributing the credit shortage and stagnation in economic activity to the reduced flow of foreign funds. In May and June some RM700 million had been raised abroad; in July, August and September, only some RM30 million. (Falkus, 1975, p. 461.)

In early 1929, a committee of experts led by O. D. Young met in Paris to work on a new schedule of German reparation payments. By that time, the flow of credits from the United States had fallen sharply. American investors had started to place their funds at home in the booming stock market, and German prospects seemed uncertain at best. As uncertainty regarding the results of the Paris conference increased, the Reichsmark was driven to the gold-export point, and the Reichsbank was forced to raise its discount rate from 6.5 to 7.5 percent and to impose rigorous credit restrictions. The Young Plan was finally put into effect in April 1930, but by that time the American stock market had collapsed and the world economy was on its way to the Depression.

The Young Plan was basically a rescheduling plan. It reduced the size of Germany's annual payments and provided a new loan of approximately RM1.2 billion ($300 million). Unlike the reschedulings of the 1980s, however, it reduced the current discounted value of the stream of reparation payments, which fell from the RM132 billion set by the Reparations Commission to about RM37 billion. The "transfer protection" system of the Dawes Plan was eliminated; Germany was made responsible for external payments as well as internal collections, and the payments had to be made in foreign exchange or gold, not in Reichsmarks. Nevertheless, the annual payments were divided into unconditional and conditional parts: the former could not be postponed, but the latter could be postponed for up to two years. The internal collection mechanisms of the Dawes Plan were abolished, apart from a special contribution to be made by the German Railway Company, amounting to RM660 million and corresponding to the unconditional annual payment. Finally, the Bank for International Settlements was created to facilitate and supervise the payment of reparations and war debts and to float the Young loan.

In 1930 Germany's industrial production declined for the first time since 1926, and real wages also fell (Table 3). A trade surplus emerged in spite of a drop in exports, thanks to a drastic restriction of imports and an improvement in the terms of trade, but it was barely large enough to cover reparations, let alone interest and amortization on Germany's loans and bonds. The annual figures still showed a net capital inflow, owing mainly to a long-term inflow in the first half of the year, which included the Young loan. In the second half of 1930, Germany was unable to float any more long-term bonds, and short-term funds began to leave the country. Germany was able to balance its payments only by short-term borrowing, and it suffered a small loss of reserves for the second year in a row (see Table 2).

In the September 1930 elections, Hitler's National Socialist Party made its presence felt, increasing the fears of potential creditors and leading to further capital flight and the withdrawal of foreign funds. Domestic finances were also getting out of control, undermining confidence in the Reichsmark. By early 1931, with domestic budget difficulties continuing and the withdrawal of foreign funds speeding up, foreign loans were virtually unobtainable (Moulton and Pasvolsky, 1932, p. 308).

In March 1931, Germany suddenly announced a customs union with Austria, generating an international political crisis that turned into a financial collapse. The collapse came first in Austria with a run on the Creditanstalt Bank in May. It spread to Germany when a run on the Reichsbank began in early June. Between May 30 and June 6, the Reichsbank's reserves declined by $38 million (see Figure 1). On June 5, the German government issued a manifesto assessing the situation and calling for a further reduction of the reparations burden. This made the financial markets even more nervous and led to a faster withdrawal of foreign funds. In the next week, reserves declined by an additional $130 million to $445 million. It was clear to all that the collapse would come very soon. But the Young Plan required ninety days' notice before any suspension of reparation payments, so the June 15 payment was duly made.

FIGURE 1

Gold and Foreign-Exchange Reserves, Reichsbank, 1928-35

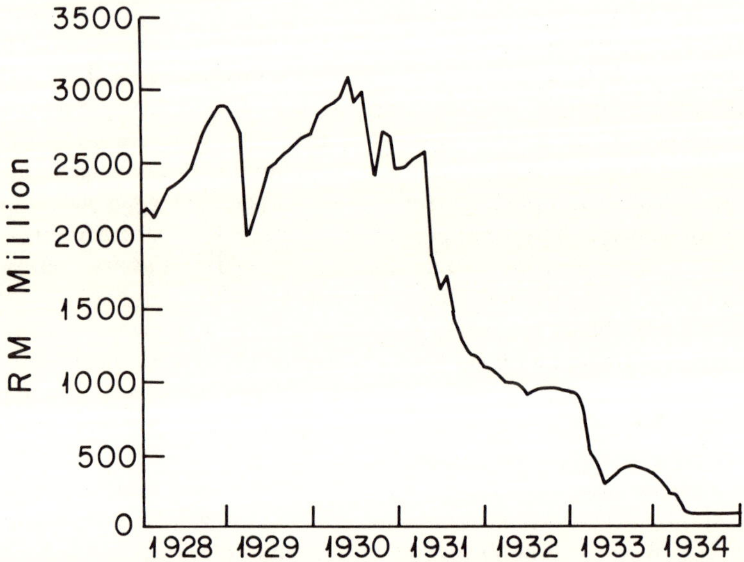

Source: Harris (1935, p. 115).

On June 18, Keynes, then in the United States and sensing the urgency of the situation, sent a cable to Hubert Henderson:

> Probable American banks continue gradually withdraw funds. Position many banks here so weak they will run no risks merely to help general situation. Moratorium or other suspension not fully discounted by banks, and announcement may make matters worse. (Keynes, 1978, pp. 354-355.)

Two days later, President Hoover announced a one-year moratorium on all war debts and reparations. But the withdrawal of foreign money from Germany continued in spite of sharp increases in the Reichsbank's discount rate. On July 13, German banks were closed for two days and foreign-exchange controls were imposed, acknowledging the final collapse. At the end of July, after a reserve loss of about RM3 million, reflecting withdrawals of foreign funds and capital flight, German short-term liabilities still totaled almost RM12 million,[3] representing about half of Germany's total indebtedness. A year later, in 1932, war debts and reparations were all but canceled in the

[3] *The Economist* (1932, p. 11). This indicates that the figures in Table 2 probably underestimate the accumulation of short-term debt.

Lausanne Settlement, but the rest of Germany's debt was serviced until 1934, when Hitler repudiated it and ended the story.

3 A Review of the Brazilian Experience, 1973-82[4]

Brazilian growth was rapid in the period that preceded the external shock in December 1973. That year marked the end of the period that became known as the "Brazilian Miracle." Between 1968 and 1973, Brazil's GDP grew at an average rate of 11 percent per year. The annual rate of inflation averaged 20 percent, but it declined over the period. Gross fixed capital formation rose from 19 to 22.4 percent of GDP, and the balance of payments seemed to pose no problem. Both exports and imports rose from around $1.9 billion in 1968 to $6.2 billion in 1973 as Brazil promoted its exports in an environment of booming world trade, creating room for the induced growth in imports. Foreign capital was plentiful, and Brazil ran balance-of-payments surpluses in every year during the period. Foreign-exchange reserves increased from $199 million at the end of 1967 to over $66 billion at the end of 1973. As Bacha and Malan (1983, p. 10) point out, foreign borrowing was a viable option because the absence of a foreign-exchange constraint allowed for high rates of investment and growth.

In addition to favorable international conditions, Brazil also benefited from high excess capacity in the early stages of the boom and from expansionary monetary and fiscal policies. Consumer and housing loans rose, and an ambitious program of public investments was launched. In 1973, the monetary base rose 47 percent, thanks to an expansion in the loans of the Banco do Brasil and to the gain in reserves. As the economy approached full capacity, however, inflationary pressures had to be repressed through price controls to meet the 12 percent inflation target.

The outlook for the Brazilian economy seemed very promising, calling for little more than some short-run fine tuning with respect to inflation and monetary expansion. Under the assumption made in early 1974 by the Second National Development Plan that the world economy would continue to boom, its optimistic targets did not seem impossible. But the world economy did not continue to boom. In December 1973, it was hit by the shock of a fivefold increase in the price of oil.

At the start of 1974, the trade balance deteriorated quickly and the money supply ran out of control. The Geisel government took office in March knowing that some adjustment would be necessary. As Mario H. Simonsen (1980, pp. 10-11), Minister of Finance under Geisel, later related,

[4] This section draws heavily on the work of Malan and Bonelli (1983), Bacha and Malan (1983), and Diaz-Alejandro (1983).

> President Geisel took office on March 15, 1974, inheriting repressed prices, a number of commodity shortages and a huge deficit in the trade balance. In his five year period a compromise solution was attempted for a number of objectives, namely: (i) to adjust the balance of payments and to keep a good international credit standing; (ii) to keep real product growing at its historical pace; (iii) to control the inflation rate within acceptable limits by Brazilian standards; (iv) to promote export growth and to reduce the foreign dependence of the country through a new program of import substitution. Times were difficult enough and objectives to reconcile also conflicting enough.

The immediate consequence of the oil shock was a $4.6 billion deterioration in the trade balance, in spite of an increase in exports. Oil imports rose from $0.7 to $2.8 billion, and nonoil imports also rose substantially. The economy was still under heavy demand stimulus, in spite of some effort to bring inflation down by reducing the growth rate of the money supply. The decision of the Geisel administration not only to continue the projects initiated in the boom period but to launch an ambitious import-substitution program that would require foreign capital is an example of the conflicting goals Simonsen referred to; balance-of-payments adjustment would be impossible in the short run because growth was given priority. The other standard adjustment tool, a real devaluation, was not even considered. Instead, a crawling peg was used to maintain the purchasing-power parity of the cruzeiro with respect to the dollar. Given the decision to avoid adjustment, the only alternative left was to go on borrowing.

In the first two years of the Geisel administration, 1974 and 1975, foreign borrowing was not large enough to cover the current-account deficit, causing a loss of reserves. This loss compounded the effects of a tight monetary policy and led to a fall in industrial production in 1974. After that, the emphasis shifted back to growth. By the end of 1976, GDP had risen by 9.7 percent and inflation was again becoming a problem. Aggregate demand had heated up, while wage indexation meant that prices would be slow to come down.

In 1977 monetary policy became tight again, this time implemented by a shift from standard monetary targets to credit ceilings. The GDP growth rate fell to 5.7 percent in 1977, leading to a fall in imports; with a favorable shift in the terms of trade, trade was balanced after three years of deficit. Investment declined from its peak of 25 percent of GDP in 1975 to 21.3 percent of GDP in 1977 (Table 4).

The next year was marked by moderate growth and falling inflation. Although the trade balance registered a $1 billion deficit in 1978, due mainly to an adverse shift in the terms of trade (Tables 4 and 5), exports had doubled in the five years after the oil shock, growing faster than world trade, while imports had been kept roughly constant. It could thus be argued that the Brazilian balance of payments had been fully adjusted to the increase in oil prices.

TABLE 4
ECONOMIC INDICATORS FOR BRAZIL

	Investment (% of GDP)	Savings (% of GDP)	Government Deficit[a] (% of GDP)	GDP Growth (%)	Inflation (%)	Real Wage	Terms of Trade
1977	21.3	20.5	n.a.	5.7	42.5	100	100
1978	21.2	19.8	n.a.	5.0	37.6	108	86
1979	20.3	18.2	3.0	6.4	55.9	110	79
1980	21.1	18.8	3.6	7.2	106.5	101	65
1981	19.2	18.7	6.0	−1.6	113.0	102	55
1982	18.4	17.4	6.6	0.9	92.0	113	54

[a] Public-sector borrowing requirement minus monetary correction on debt. This is basically an inflation-adjusted government deficit.

SOURCE: *Conjuntura Economica*, June 1984; International Monetary Fund; Modiano (1983) for real wages.

As many economists have pointed out, however, this was not entirely true. Medium- and long-term net foreign debt had grown from $6 to $32 billion by the end of 1977, most of it contracted at floating interest rates. In 1978, before the second oil shock, the current-account deficit was already more than half the size of total exports (Table 5), mainly because of a 2 percentage point jump in international interest rates. Moreover, the volume of oil imports *increased* by a third between 1973 and 1978 as oil prices declined in real terms.

Allowing the Brazilian economy to become increasingly vulnerable to rises in interest rates and oil prices may have been justified, given its performance, but adjustment could not be postponed forever. A real devaluation was not attempted. In addition, Brazilians had little or no incentive to reduce oil consumption, because the domestic prices of oil subproducts were heavily subsidized throughout the Geisel term. Finally, as in the case of Germany, there were serious questions about the feasibility of some of the investment projects undertaken, such as the atomic energy and gasohol programs.

The second oil shock in early 1979 came as an additional reminder that things could go sour. In spite of tighter monetary and credit policies, inflation had not come down significantly in 1978, mainly because of adverse supply shocks and the cost-push effect of lagged wage indexation. When oil prices started to rise, the need for economic adjustment became even clearer. When President Figueiredo took office on March 15, 1979, and brought Mario H. Simonsen with him, this time as Planning Minister, they gave priority to combatting inflation.

In August 1979, however, Simonsen resigned because of widespread polit-

TABLE 5
BRAZIL'S BALANCE OF PAYMENTS
(in millions of dollars)

	1978	1979	1980	1981	1982
Exports	12,659	15,244	20,132	23,293	20,175
Imports	−13,683	−18,084	−22,955	−22,091	−19,395
Trade balance	−1,024	−2,840	−2,823	1,202	780
Interest payments (net)	−2,696	−4,185	−6,311	−9,161	−11,353
Reinvested profits (net)	−975	−721	−411	−741	−1,556
Other services (net)	−2,295	−2,996	−3,262	−3,035	−4,182
Current account	−6,990	−10,742	−12,807	−11,735	−16,311
Direct investments [a]	2,046	2,212	1,532	2,326	2,547
Long-term loans	14,284	11,907	11,513	17,423	14,881
Amortization payments	−5,439	−6,5451	−6,706	−7,515	−8,234
Short-term capital (net)	1,394	1,120	3,358	1,598	−797
Brazilian lending	−357	−608	−27	−921	−594
Capital account	11,928	8,090	9,670	12,911	7,803
Errors and omissions	−639	−130	−343	−414	−368
Gold monetization and valuation adjustments	253	599	376	−331	285
Change in monetary liabilities	87	−113	237	76	4,335 [b]
Change in gross official reserves [loss = (−)]	4,639	−2,296	−2,867	507	−4,256

[a] Includes "reinvested profits."
[b] Includes bridge loan of U.S. $2,339 million.
SOURCE: International Monetary Fund.

ical opposition to his stabilization effort. His place was taken by Antonio Delfim Netto, the well-known Minister of Economics during the "Brazilian miracle" of 1968-73. Delfim believed that the inflation and balance-of-payments problems should be solved by promoting growth, particularly agricultural growth. This, he expected, would lead to a fall in domestic inflation and to a trade surplus, all at the small cost of subsidies and minimum-price guarantees, financed by monetary expansion. As a consequence, the monetary base grew 64 percent in 1979, compared with 45 percent in the previous year.

There were also strong inflationary pressures on the cost side. In November a new wage law was enacted that reduced the lag in wage indexation to six months and gave low-paid workers wage increases in excess of past inflation. In December the cruzeiro was devalued by 30 percent in terms of the dollar, export subsidies were reduced, and import restrictions were relaxed. Inflation jumped to almost 80 percent on an end-of-period basis, and foreign confidence in Brazil began to fade. On December 15, 1979, *The Economist* (p. 69) was already saying that Brazil might be forced to borrow from the International Monetary Fund during the next year.

The balance of payments showed a deficit of $2.3 billion in 1979, as imports increased by 32 percent, world interest rates continued to climb, the world went into a recession, and capital inflows fell by 32 percent (Table 5). A small balance-of-payments crisis took place in the winter of 1979-80; it is reflected in the switch from long- to short-term financing of the current-account deficit (Table 6). Hoping to have some impact on inflationary expectations, Delfim announced at the end of 1979 that monetary correction (the lagged indexation factor) would be limited to 45 percent in 1980 and the rate of devaluation vis-à-vis the dollar would be limited to 40 percent. Inflation continued to rise in the first half of 1980, however, and these targets were eventually abandoned. Nevertheless, the cumulative devaluation of the cruzeiro in 1980 remained below the cruzeiro/dollar inflation differential, so that the effect of the 1979 devaluation was substantially reduced by the end of 1980 (Figure 2).

The combination of fast growth at home and a world recession led to $4.8 billion increases in both exports and imports, keeping the trade deficit at $2.8 billion for the second year in a row (Table 5). In addition, international interest rates reacted to monetary contraction in the United States by rising 3 percentage points, causing Brazil's current account to deteriorate by $2 billion. *The Economist* (Sept. 6, 1980, pp. 78-79) announced that Brazil was "crashing through the debt barrier," and that "many banks [are] reaching their 'country limit' for Brazil and the flood of new lenders has dried up. . . ." In the absence of capital controls, a more violent balance-of-payments crisis would probably have occurred, driving reserves to zero. In the event, net foreign debt rose from $48.4 to $58.9 billion, including a significant $3.4 billion increase in short-term liabilities and a $3.0 billion reserve loss (Table 7).

TABLE 6
BRAZIL'S CURRENT-ACCOUNT FINANCING
(in millions of dollars)

	Current Account	Long-Term Financing[a]	Short-Term Financing[b]	Gross Reserve Loss
1979:1	−2,251	1,476	−280	811
2	−2,247	1,461	350	1,193
3	−2,952	1,661	−51	1,084
4	−3,292	2,210	829	238
1980:1	−3,649	734	1,335	2,157
2	−3,183	1,619	162	1,505
3	−3,505	2,077	543	334
4	−2,470	2,529	679	−489
1981:1	−2,870	1,664	913	503
2	−3,077	2,788	−350	298
3	−3,116	2,993	−177	−144
4	−2,671	4,258	842	−1,308
1982:1	−3,640	1,117	1,818	455
2	−4,181	3,038	758	803
3	−4,493	2,503	−125	1,698
4	−3,996	1,257	−2,515	1,317[c]

[a] Net long-term loans plus direct investment.

[b] Net short-term loans.

[c] Without the bridge loan and other emergency measures, the loss would have been at least $4 billion higher.

NOTE: Gold revaluations are not taken into account, as they are in Table 5.

SOURCE: *Boletim do Banco Central do Brasil*, various issues.

A trip to the IMF was certainly in the cards, but Delfim tried to deal a different hand. He tried at first to salvage his original strategy, the pursuit of adjustment through growth, then opted for what *The Economist* called a "course correction," acknowledging that he had "more or less exhausted the banks' willingness to lend his country money—until Brazil is back in the black" (Nov. 29, 1980, p. 61). The targets for monetary and exchange-rate corrections were formally abandoned, interest rates were decontrolled, and a 5 percent target for GDP growth was announced for 1981. A very tight monetary policy was implemented to achieve this objective, as documented, for example, in Bacha (1983, pp. 330-332). Economic activity declined sharply; instead of growing at 5 percent, GDP fell 1.6 percent.

In spite of a deterioration in the terms of trade, the trade balance improved by $4 billion, moving into surplus. Bankers were reported to be "looking hap-

FIGURE 2

THE REAL TRADE-WEIGHTED EXCHANGE RATE, BRAZIL, 1979-84

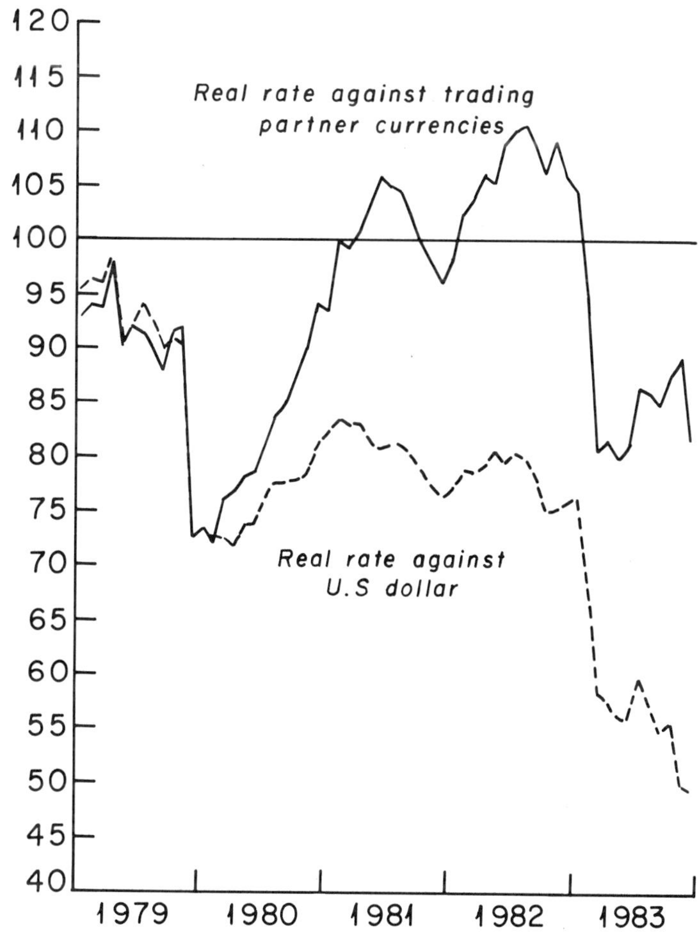

NOTE: Increases represent appreciations of the cruzeiro.
SOURCE: International Monetary Fund.

pier by the hour" as Brazil was "deflating its way out of the deficit" (*The Economist*, June 20, 1981). This effort, however, was not paying off, because world interest rates continued to climb, to an annual average of 18.9 percent, raising debt-service costs. The current account improved only slightly, and bankers found themselves lending the amounts necessary to cover the remaining def-

TABLE 7
BRAZIL'S FOREIGN DEBT AND RESERVES
(in millions of dollars)

	Medium and Long-Term Foreign Debt	Short-Term Foreign Debt [a]	Official Monetary Liabilities [b]	Total Foreign Liabilities	Gross Reserves [c]	Net Official Reserves [d]
1977	32,037	2,703	1,512 [e]	34,252	7,256	5,744
1978	43,511	4,097	1,599 [e]	49,207	11,894	10,295
1979	49,904	5,217	1,486 [e]	56,607	9,688	8,202
1980	53,848	8,575	1,723	64,146	6,912	5,189
1981	61,411	10,173	1,799	73,383	7,507	5,708
1982	69,654	9,376 [f]	6,134	85,164	3,250	−2,884
1983	81,319	7,554	7,106	95,979	3,757	−3,349

[a] Data derived from the annual balance-of-payment flow, Table 5 above.
[b] Basis is 1980 IMF number.
[c] Foreign exchange, gold, SDRs, and reserve position in the IMF.
[d] Gross reserves minus official monetary liabilities.
[e] May overstate true values.
[f] From "standard, non-registered" debt given in the central bank's annual report.
SOURCE: International Monetary Fund and central bank.

icit. Little adjustment took place; the cruzeiro remained overvalued and inflation rose slightly. The stage was set for the final stretch.

The domestic liquidity crunch continued into 1982. Interest rates on consumer loans and working capital remained very high, and the cruzeiro appreciated even further in real terms, as it followed the appreciating dollar. Although imports were still kept very low, the trade balance did not improve, because exports dropped in response to a severe contraction in world trade. In the first quarter of 1982, a sharp reversal in the pattern of financing took place, as it had two years before. Long-term loans dropped substantially, and the gap was filled by short-term loans obtained mostly through the interbank market. Investment continued to decline, falling to 18.4 percent of GDP in 1982, and economic activity was still depressed. In the first half of 1982, capital flows were insufficient to finance the growing current-account deficit, and reserves fell to $1.2 billion. Brazil was still on its feet, but it might not have been able to stay upright even in the absence of an international liquidity crisis.

When the Mexican collapse came in August 1982, all doubt disappeared. Capital flows to Brazil contracted sharply and reserves fell further. Complaints came from government and business that the Mexican debt crisis was undermining Brazil's ability to address its own balance-of-payments problems, but they were not made loudly. The government was trying to put on a good show in order to do well in the forthcoming November elections. It decided not to suspend debt service and rejected a trip to the IMF, claiming that Brazil could solve its own problems. As indicated by the quarterly balance-of-payments figures shown in Table 6, this would turn out to be impossible.

A sharp reversal in short-term capital flows took place after the Mexican crisis, as well as another reduction in long-term loans. In the last quarter of 1982 alone, the capital account showed an *outflow* of $1.3 billion, and the overall balance of payments showed a deficit of $5.7 billion. The situation would have been even worse if capital flows had not been under strict control, but it was bad enough. Brazil had to call for help in meeting its payments. An emergency package was put together by the banks, the IMF, the U.S. Treasury, and the Bank for International Settlements, leading to an overall increase of $4.3 billion in Brazil's official monetary liabilities in 1982. Net reserves crashed from $5.7 billion at the end of 1981 to *minus* $2.9 billion at the end of 1982—a balance-of-payments collapse.

4 Germany and Brazil Compared

Size and Nature of the External Shocks

The German economy was burdened with reparation payments from 1919, when the Treaty of Versailles was signed, to the Hoover moratorium in 1931. After an apparently successful period of externally financed growth, Germany was caught by the Depression and a crisis was inevitable. With some qualifications, we can tell a similar story about Brazil in the late 1970s and early 1980s. In 1973 the Brazilian economy was hit by a large exogenous oil shock, which was followed by a period of growth-with-debt similar to Germany's. After that, a combination of many factors, including higher oil prices and interest rates, low levels of world economic activity and trade, and domestic mismanagement, led to a crisis in the last quarter of 1982. Thus, external shocks, broadly defined, played key explanatory roles in the eventual balance-of-payments crises of both countries.

Going beyond this qualitative similarity, it is natural to ask whether the shocks that hit Germany and Brazil were of comparable magnitude. To answer this question I follow Machlup's (1964) approach. He suggests that the increased current-account burden be compared with GDP and exports. The ratio to GDP measures the extent of the domestic budgetary problem—the required domestic fund raising and burden sharing. The ratio to exports indicates the magnitude of the transfer problem—the required conversion of domestic funds into an acceptable international means of payment. These measures, for which the ratios are presented in Table 8, suffer from a number of shortcomings, but they serve as a first approximation.

TABLE 8

TRANSFER BURDENS

(in percent)

	Ratio to GDP (*A/Y*)	Ratio to Exports (*A/X*)
Germany:		
1925-28	1.9	13.2
1929-31	3.5	14.6
Brazil:		
1974-78	1.8	26.7
1979-82	2.5	29.8

Germany:

A = annual average of reparations in period.

Y = national-income estimates for 1925 and 1929 from Machlup (1964, p. 383).

X = annual average of exports.

Brazil:

A = annual average of oil imports in excess of 1973 (for 1974-78) or 1978 (for 1979-82).

Y = annual average of GDP.

X = annual average of exports.

For Germany, the period is divided into two subperiods, 1925-28, a period of balance-of-payments surpluses, and 1929-31. Since national-income estimates are available only for 1925, 1929, and 1932, the German numbers in Table 8 must be taken as very rough approximations. In order to minimize distortions and still be able to differentiate between periods, the 1925 and 1929 figures were used for the national-income ratios instead of the period averages used for the export ratios.

For Brazil, the two subperiods were 1974-78 and 1979-82. Because the adjustment that took place in 1974-78 was insufficient, the figures for the second subperiod may underestimate the actual burden. (This bias is compounded by the use of 1978 oil imports for the second subperiod, but their use is justified for another reason, advanced below.)

The nature of the shocks must also be taken into account before we can conclude that Germany and Brazil faced similar burdens. In particular, as Marion and Swensson (1984) have so elegantly shown, distinctions between anticipated and unanticipated changes and between temporary and permanent changes imply different optimal dynamic responses to shocks.

The case of reparations is the easiest. It is probably fair to say that after World War I began, German taxpayers attached a certain probability to a German defeat. As a consequence, the payment of reparations must have been at least partly anticipated. But, with Germany at war, they were unlikely to adjust optimally to that possibility. Thus, reparations had almost the effect of an unanticipated shock.

The case of the oil shocks is more complex, so I call upon Gately's (1984) survey for help. The average view quoted there characterizes the first oil shock as largely unanticipated but as permanent in the sense that the price of oil was not expected to return to its pre-1974 level. The second oil shock was again a partial surprise, and it had the effect of reinforcing the view that the first shock had been permanent. The price elasticity of demand for oil must also be considered. It is usually taken to be very low in the short and medium run. In the case of Brazil, we saw that no adjustment in oil consumption took place because the domestic price of oil was heavily subsidized. There was some adjustment on the supply side, as domestic oil production increased by 24 percent from 1973 to 1982. (It was to account for this adjustment that 1978 oil imports were used to measure the second-period burden.)

On the whole, it appears that Germany and Brazil faced similar qualitative problems. Quantitatively, the burdens to GDP were comparable, but the relationships to exports differed to the extent that Germany was a more open economy. The increase in Brazilian oil payments was considerably larger relative to exports than were German reparation payments relative to exports.

Short-Run Adjustment

The degree of short-run adjustment in the two countries can be compared by examining some important macroeconomic variables in each country. (The dynamic long-run process is considered in section 5.)

The standard short-run tools for adjustment to an adverse balance-of-payments shock are devaluation of the currency and reduction of domestic absorption. A real devaluation also requires a fall in real wages measured in terms of traded goods. In both episodes considered here, real wages rose in the period following the first external shock. This suggests that no real adjustment took place until the economies were hit for the second time, when real wages fell. The classical Hume-Mill adjustment process, which relies on the flexibility of wages and prices, was never given a chance to operate, since both countries opted to finance the shocks rather than try to reduce real wages. One can conjecture, however, that under union pressure in the case of Germany and wage indexation in the case of Brazil, early adjustment would have been just as costly as tardy adjustment turned out to be.

The other standard adjustment tool, domestic contraction, was also avoided. In Germany there was significant political pressure to restore the economy to its pre-war level, and in Brazil there was pressure for economic development. In response, both governments ran budget deficits to accommodate the external shocks and avoid adjustment. In both countries, moreover, there was a tendency to finance long-term projects with short-term loans, a fact that accounted in part for the increase in vulnerability that preceded both crises.

The two countries differed greatly in their use of inflation to finance the budget deficits. Because Germany was on the gold-exchange standard, the budget deficits were financed by domestic and foreign borrowing, and inflation was never a problem. In Brazil, which was under no such constraint, a large proportion of the budget deficit was monetized.

Although exchange-rate adjustment did not play an important role in Germany under the gold-exchange standard, the Reichsmark appreciated slightly in real terms; the nominal exchange rate was fixed between 1926 and 1930, but the majority of Germany's trading partners deflated more than Germany did (League of Nations, 1931, p. 92). Brazil's trade-weighted real exchange rate remained roughly constant from 1973 to 1978, again indicating no adjustment; thereafter, however, the cruzeiro appreciated substantially in real terms, despite the devaluation of December 1979. This move was perverse, given the balance-of-payments situation. It was caused at first by the policy of fixing the devaluation rate at low levels, and later by the policy of maintaining the real dollar rate constant when the dollar was appreciating.

Two other factors, weak trade structure and volatile capital flows, point to important similarities. Germany was heavily dependent on imported raw materials and foodstuffs to produce its manufactured exports. Brazil is constrained in much the same way; it depends on imported capital goods and oil to maintain its production of manufactured goods, which account for more than half its exports. And the volatility of capital flows was important, if not decisive, in explaining economic fluctuations in both countries.

The Paths toward Collapse

As we have seen, both countries decided to borrow after being hit by the initial shocks, in order to postpone adjustment. Germany had enjoyed a booming economy before World War I and was under strong domestic pressure to regain its previous standard of living. In any case, a period of trade deficits was clearly needed to finance investment because of the overall state of the economy and its trade structure. Brazil made a similar move after the first oil shock, starting a number of large investment projects, perhaps in the hope that the shock was temporary. These were very long-term projects, and the expectation of continuing capital inflows was a key determinant of the decision not to adjust. Real interest rates were very low at that time and were expected to remain low for as long as the savings of the oil-exporting countries applied pressure on financial markets. As many have pointed out, both countries made gambles, but not unreasonable ones given the structures of their economies and the potentially high costs of rapid adjustment. There were other costs attached to the gambles, however, in the form of increased vulnerability to further shocks.

The two economies followed somewhat different paths when faced with a second round of problems. In Germany, the second shock was the slowdown and subsequent reversal of foreign capital flows. The Great Depression began shortly after that shock, and Germany was forced to adjust by restricting domestic activity and curbing imports. Even if Germany had been granted some debt relief or had rescheduled its payments, it could not have avoided a fall in domestic activity, because its export markets had contracted sharply.

Brazil, by contrast, had a choice after oil prices went up for the second time and interest rates started to rise. Foreign funds were still available, and Delfim opted to postpone (or avoid) adjustment. This was a crucial mistake. The standard theory of optimal borrowing tells us that an economy should finance temporary shocks and adjust to permanent ones. The second oil shock should have been taken to mean that Brazil would continue to confront high oil prices, and some adjustment should have been initiated. In addition, these shocks hit an economy with an already substantial volume of foreign debt and drove the transfer burden to unprecedently high levels.

As interest rates continued to rise and the world went into recession, it finally became clear to the authorities that adjustment would be necessary. The decision to switch gears came late and involved mainly domestic contraction. The exchange rate was not used as an instrument, but the trade balance improved in large part because of excellent export performance in 1981. After this interval, however, the picture again began to resemble Germany's. The adjustment at home extracted a heavy toll from the economy, and the shrinking inflow of foreign capital became a binding constraint.

5 Overborrowing and Overlending

In the crises analyzed above, the causal chain involved the compounding of exogenous shocks and policy mistakes. Both countries underadjusted to the initial external disturbances, becoming vulnerable to further shocks. Since the underadjustment was made possible by foreign loans, let us evaluate the behavior of borrowers and lenders and their roles in the two episodes.

The Behavior of Borrowers

Following Gersovitz (1984), we can say that countries borrow (a) to smooth consumption when faced with temporary fluctuations in income, (b) to invest, (c) to smooth adjustment, and (d) to finance trade. The first two reasons come directly from standard models of optimal borrowing, which tell us to equate the discounted marginal utilities of future consumption and to invest until the marginal product of capital equals the marginal cost of capital. The last two reasons have not been fully analyzed in formal models but are quite intuitive. With reference to smoothing adjustment, in particular, the benefits from full and immediate adjustment to a permanent shock have to be balanced against the costs of adjusting. Such costs could arise from the short-run rigidities discussed above and from costly intersectoral reallocations of capital, among other causes.

What then can we say about Germany and Brazil? Since these countries apparently borrowed for all of these reasons, let us examine them one at a time. Smoothing consumption was certainly not a valid reason for either country to borrow, because both reparations and higher oil prices were long-lasting shocks. The investment motive is perhaps the hardest of all to analyze, because we need information about prospective profitability. In principle, the volume of borrowing for investment that took place in Germany and Brazil was probably justified by the opportunities that existed; in practice, many projects were poorly chosen. The adjustment motive makes sense if it serves to reduce the speed of adjustment but does not postpone adjustment completely. In the case of Germany, it seems that very little or no adjustment took place from 1924 to 1928, so we can conclude that there was some overborrowing. In Brazil, some adjustment took place between 1974 and 1979, although it turned out *ex post* to have been inadequate to the need. For the eighteen months starting in August 1979, however, there was no excuse for borrowing without adjustment. Borrowing to finance trade was valid for both countries, but only up to a certain point. Germany used short-term loans to finance working capital and longer-run projects. Anecdotal evidence from Brazil indicates that, starting with the mini-crisis of 1980, trade and other short-term credit lines were being used to finance the balance of payments. Needless to say, these financing strategies were inappropriate. One is led to conclude that some overborrowing and underadjustment took place in both Germany and Brazil.

The Behavior of Lenders

Why did the matching overlending take place? Guttentag and Herring (1984) provide us with a number of explanations: (a) what they call "disaster myopia," a phenomenon that may cause economic agents to underestimate the probability of a rare but disastrous event, such as a debt default; (b) imperfect information and faulty analyses of loans, reflecting an inadequate data base, an inadequate analysis of covariances, belief in the "short-leash" fallacy, which implies that short maturities allow banks to recall loans, and a misemphasis on accounting values, all of which lead banks to misassess the risks involved; and (c) the incentive effects of deposit insurance and an implicit belief in a bailout should a crisis occur. This last is the standard "moral hazard" argument that leads to excessive risk taking. It also helps explain the so-called "herd behavior" of banks, which tend to take on similar exposures in the belief that the industry as a whole will not be allowed to go under.

To Guttentag and Herring's explanations of overlending I add two more: (d) failure to consider project risk, and (e) failure to consider country or foreign-exchange risk. Every international loan has both, the "project risk" being unique to each individual borrower, and the country or foreign-exchange risk being related to macroeconomic conditions and increasing with the sum of microrisks. Diaz-Alejandro (1984, p. 12) provides a very interesting example of the influence of project risk. After a large bailout operation in 1977, all loans to private borrowers in Chile were guaranteed *de facto* by the government, so that project risk could be ignored. This compounded the effect of Chile's exchange-rate policies and led to massive capital inflows. The role of country risk can be interpreted as an externality: if each individual lender is small and takes the macrorisk as given or ignores the contribution of its own loan to that risk, then the overall level of loans will be excessive.

Let us now apply these explanations to lending behavior in the German and Brazilian cases.

In Germany, one large component of capital inflows took the form of bond placements in New York facilitated by the Dawes loan. Mintz (1951, pp. 70-71) and C. Lewis (1938, p. 376) point out that investors were attracted to the higher yields offered by low-grade foreign bonds, unaware of the risks involved. There were no defaults on foreign government bonds during the period, and the confidence of the public grew as time passed and no losses were incurred. This pattern points to the roles of disaster myopia and imperfect information in the assessment of loan risks. It is hard, however, to blame individual bond holders for their judgment, so we must turn to the behavior of intermediaries.

The behavior of banking houses is somewhat puzzling. On the one hand, they were overly optimistic and backward-looking in their expectations; on the other hand, they were not ignorant of the main risk factors. Mintz (1951, pp. 74-77), for example, shows that though the banks made careful credit analyses, they "took little account of the probability that these favorable trends were unlikely to continue." This happened in spite of repeated warnings by well-known authorities like Moulton (1924) and S. Parker Gilbert, the Agent General for Reparation Payments (quoted by Mintz, 1951, p. 77). These authorities pointed out at the time that Germany was overborrowing and overspending and that the prospects of its paying reparations were bleak, not to mention amortizing subsequent loans. Indeed, the bankers did worse than ignore the advice of experts: they retaliated against economists like Harold Moulton, who argued against excessive loans to Germany, by cutting their research funds.[5] One is led to conclude that the major banks were deliberately dumping these risky loans on the poorly informed public and smaller banks. This conclusion is reinforced by the fact that the large metropolitan banks held virtually no German bonds in their portfolios.[6]

The large banks did hold short-term loans, the other large component of capital flows to Germany. Here the explanation must come from the externality theory outlined above:

> In many cases the loan investigators apparently ignored the relationships between new issues and the amounts of foreign capital already invested in the borrowing country. For example, when loans were extended to German banks the lenders carefully analyzed the statement of the particular borrower, but in many cases did not take account of the total of Germany's foreign obligations. Yet it was the enormous total of the country's foreign indebtedness, and not the borrowing of any particular bank, that was responsible for the standstill agreements between the German banks and their foreign creditors. (C. Lewis, 1938, pp. 405-406.)

The same argument was put forth in a slightly different context to criticize the excesses of competitive foreign lending:

> [A] serious objection to highly competitive bidding for foreign loans is that it ordinarily leads to the distribution of the foreign financing of a country (including loans of the national government, political subdivisions, and corporations) among a large number of banking firms. The situation tends to obscure overborrowing by the country as a whole. Each banking house considers primarily the credit standing of the borrower with which it is dealing, and there is a tendency to overlook the effect on the country as a whole of loans obtained by other borrowers. Thus, each individual loan may be warranted by the financial position of the borrower, but the service on the entire external debt may be in excess of the capacity of the country to transfer the funds abroad in a period of depression. (Madden, Nadler, and Sauvain, 1937, pp. 222-223.)

Now let us examine the behavior of Brazil's creditors. As we have seen, Brazil financed high rates of growth by external bank loans from 1968 to 1973, the miracle years. It was therefore only natural that the impact of the first oil shock was almost automatically financed, in what was seen as successful recycling. But after that, some adjustment should have taken place. Instead, more loans were provided and a large proportion of them was guaranteed by the Brazilian government, giving lenders a false sense of security. Each individually guaranteed loan was safe, but all loans put together were not, because Brazil did not adjust. This became clear *ex post*, when it was discovered

[5] See Ferguson (1984, p. 76). Moulton went on to establish The Brookings Institution.

[6] See U.S. Senate (1931). In particular, C. Mitchell testified (p. 80) that the National City Bank held less than 0.01 percent of its assets in the form of long-term German bonds, and O. H. Kahn testified (pp. 134-142) that Kuhn, Loeb & Co. held no such bonds and that, in order to remain liquid, all the larger metropolitan banks, acting as merchant banks, probably followed the same practice.

that much of the borrowing was done by state-owned enterprises, which were following orders to borrow in order to finance Brazil's balance of payments.

The argument can be summarized in terms of three of the five explanations of overlending given above. The first two are explanations (c), the moral hazard or incentive problem related to the provision of government guarantees, and (e), the externality related to the overall exposure of the country. The former implies that many loans were improper from a microeconomic standpoint, whereas the latter implies that the sum of all loans was excessive from a macro standpoint. A third explanation is related to (b), imperfect or incomplete information regarding the banks' total exposure to Brazil. Anecdotal evidence indicates that, after the 1982 Mexican crisis, many banks were surprised to learn how high their aggregate lending to Brazil had been. This last explanation supplements the externality argument.

Thus, we can conclude that bank overlending to Brazil had the same roots as bank overlending to Germany: banks ignored the effects of their individual actions on the overall level of risk or the vulnerability of the economy.

6 Concluding Remarks

I have argued that the experiences of Germany and Brazil were marked by a number of similarities. The two stories can be easily summarized: after being hit by an external shock, both countries underadjusted and overborrowed abroad. As a consequence, they became vulnerable to further shocks and eventually faced balance-of-payments crises.

My diagnosis of overborrowing is based on the failure of both countries to adjust their economies when faced with permanent disturbances. No budgetary discipline was imposed, and the currency was not devalued in real terms. Instead, the economy was financed with foreign credit, a large proportion of it in short-term loans. The resulting financial vulnerability explains the sudden nature of the final crises.

The behavior of lenders was likewise similar. In both cases, the failure of individual lenders to take into account the impact of their own loans on overall country risk may suffice to explain the overlending that took place.

The main lesson to be drawn from these experiences is quite simple. Countries faced with permanent disturbances should adjust as soon as possible, and lenders should keep this in mind before increasing their exposure.

References

Aldcroft, Derek H., *From Versailles to Wall Street, 1919-1929*, Berkeley, University of California Press, 1977.

Angell, James W., *The Recovery of Germany*, 1932, reprinted Westport, Conn., Greenwood Press, 1972.

Bacha, Edmar, "Vicissitudes of Recent Stabilization Attempts in Brazil and the IMF Alternative," in John Williamson, ed., *IMF Conditionality*, Washington, Institute for International Economics, 1983.

Bacha, Edmar L., and Pedro S. Malan, "Brazil's Debt: From the Miracle to the Fund," Rio de Janeiro, Catholic University, 1983, unpublished.

Balderston, T., "The Beginning of the Depression in Germany, 1927-30: Investment and the Capital Market," *Economic History Review*, 36 (August 1983), pp. 395-415.

Bresciani-Turroni, Constantino, *The Economics of Inflation*, 1937, reprinted New York, Augustus Kelley, 1968.

Bry, Gerhard, *Wages in Germany, 1881-1945*, Princeton, N.J., Princeton University Press, 1960.

Diaz-Alejandro, Carlos F., "Good-Bye Financial Repression, Hello Financial Crash," New York, Columbia University, 1984, unpublished.

———, "Some Aspects of the 1982-83 Brazilian Payments Crisis," *Brookings Papers on Economic Activity* (1983:2), pp. 515-542.

The Economist, "Reparations and War Debts," supplement, Jan. 23, 1932.

Falkus, M. E., "The German Business Cycle in the 1920s," *Economic History Review*, 28 (August 1975), pp. 451-465.

Ferguson, Thomas, "From Normalcy to New Deal: Industrial Structure, Party Competition, and American Public Policy in the Great Depression," *International Organization*, 38 (Winter 1984), pp. 41-94.

Fraga, Arminio, *Essays in International Lending and Adjustment*, Princeton, N.J., Princeton University, 1985, Ph.D. dissertation.

Gately, Dermot, "A Ten-Year Retrospective: OPEC and the World Oil Market," *Journal of Economic Literature*, 22 (September 1984), pp. 1100-1114.

Gersovitz, Mark, "Banks' International Lending Decisions: What We Know and Implications for Future Research," Princeton, N.J., Princeton University, 1984, unpublished.

Guttentag, Jack M., and Richard Herring, "Commercial Bank Lending to Less Developed Countries: From Overlending to Underlending to Structural Reform," Philadelphia, The Wharton School, 1984, unpublished.

Harris, C. R. S., *Germany's Foreign Indebtedness*, 1935, reprinted New York, Arno, 1978.

Keynes, John Maynard, *The Economic Consequences of the Peace*, London, Harcourt, Brace and Howe, 1919.

Keynes, John Maynard, *Activities 1922-1932: The End of Reparations, Collected Writings*, Vol. 18, London, Macmillan.

Kindleberger, Charles P., *Economic Response*, Cambridge, Mass., Harvard University Press, 1978.

———, *A Financial History of Western Europe*, London, Allen & Unwin, 1984.

League of Nations, *The Course and Phases of the World Economic Depression*, Geneva, 1931.

Lewis, Cleona, *America's Stake in International Investments*, Washington, The Brookings Institution, 1983.

Lewis, W. Arthur, *Economic Survey, 1919-1939*, London, Allen & Unwin, 1949.

Machlup, Fritz, "The Transfer Problem: Theme and Four Variations," in *International Payments, Debts, and Gold*, New York, Scribners, 1964.

Madden, J. T., M. Nadler, and H. C. Sauvain, *America's Experience as a Creditor Nation*, New York, Prentice-Hall, 1937.

Malan, Pedro S., and Regis Bonelli, "Crescimento Econômico, Industrialização e Balanço de Pagamentos: O Brasil dos Anos 70 aos anos 80," Rio de Janeiro, Catholic University, 1983, unpublished.

Marion, Nancy P., and Lars E. O. Swensson, "Adjustment to Expected and Unexpected Oil Price Changes," *Canadian Journal of Economics*, 17 (February 1984), pp. 15-31.

Mayer, Arno J., *Politics and Diplomacy of Peacemaking*, New York, Knopf, 1967.

Mintz, Ilse, *Deterioration in the Quality of Foreign Bonds Issued in the United States, 1920-1930*, 1951, reprinted New York, Arno, 1978.

Modiano, Eduardo M., "Choques Externos e Preços Internos: Dificuldades da Politica de Ajuste," in P. Arida, ed., *Divida Externa, Recessão e Ajuste Estrutural*, Rio de Janeiro, Paz e Terra, 1982.

Moulton, Harold G., *The Reparation Plan*, New York, McGraw-Hill, 1924.

Moulton, Harold G., and Leo Pasvolsky, *War Debts and World Prosperity*, Washington, The Brookings Institution, 1932.

Sargent, T., "The Ends of Four Big Inflations," in S. Fischer, ed., *Inflation*, Chicago, University of Chicago Press, 1983.

Simonsen, Mario H., "Inflation and Anti-Inflationary Policies in Brazil," paper presented at a conference on world inflation and indexation in Brazil, Rio de Janeiro, Getulio Vargas Foundation, 1980.

U.S. Senate, Committee on Finance, *Hearings on the Sale of Foreign Bonds or Securities in the U.S.*, S. Res. 19, Washington, 1931.

PUBLICATIONS OF THE INTERNATIONAL FINANCE SECTION

Notice to Contributors

The International Finance Section publishes at irregular intervals papers in four series: ESSAYS IN INTERNATIONAL FINANCE, PRINCETON STUDIES IN INTERNATIONAL FINANCE, SPECIAL PAPERS IN INTERNATIONAL ECONOMICS, and REPRINTS IN INTERNATIONAL FINANCE. ESSAYS and STUDIES are confined to subjects in international finance. SPECIAL PAPERS are surveys of the literature suitable for courses in colleges and universities.

An ESSAY should be a lucid exposition of a theme, accessible not only to the professional economist but to other interested readers. It should therefore avoid technical terms, should eschew mathematics and statistical tables (except when essential for an understanding of the text), and should rarely have footnotes.

A STUDY or SPECIAL PAPER may be more technical. It may include statistics and algebra and may have many footnotes. STUDIES and SPECIAL PAPERS may also be longer than ESSAYS; indeed, these two series are meant to accommodate manuscripts too long for journal articles and too short for books.

To facilitate prompt evaluation, please submit three copies of your manuscript. Retain one for your files. The manuscript should be typed on one side of 8½ by 11 strong white paper. All material should be double-spaced—text, excerpts, footnotes, tables, references, and figure legends. For more complete guidance, prospective contributors should send for the Section's style guide before preparing their manuscripts.

How to Obtain Publications

A mailing list is maintained for free distribution of all new publications to college, university, and public libraries and nongovernmental, nonprofit research institutions.

Individuals and organizations not qualifying for free distribution can obtain ESSAYS and REPRINTS as issued and announcements of new STUDIES and SPECIAL PAPERS by paying a fee of $12 (within U.S.) or $15 (outside U.S.) to cover the period January 1 through December 31, 1986. Alternatively, for $30 they can receive all publications automatically—SPECIAL PAPERS and STUDIES as well as ESSAYS and REPRINTS.

ESSAYS and REPRINTS can also be ordered from the Section at $4.50 per copy, and STUDIES and SPECIAL PAPERS at $6.50. Payment MUST be included with the order and MUST be made in U.S. dollars. PLEASE INCLUDE $1 FOR POSTAGE AND HANDLING. (These charges are waived on orders from persons or organizations in countries whose foreign-exchange regulations prohibit such remittances.) For airmail delivery outside U.S., Canada, and Mexico, there is an additional charge of $1.

All manuscripts, correspondence, and orders should be addressed to:

International Finance Section
Department of Economics, Dickinson Hall
Princeton University
Princeton, New Jersey 08544

Subscribers should notify the Section promptly of a change of address, giving the old address as well as the new one.

List of Recent Publications

Some earlier issues are still in print. Write the Section for information.

ESSAYS IN INTERNATIONAL FINANCE

130. Franco Modigliani and Tommaso Padoa-Schioppa, *The Management of an Open Economy with "100% Plus" Wage Indexation*. (Dec. 1978)
131. H. Robert Heller and Malcolm Knight, *Reserve-Currency Preferences of Central Banks*. (Dec. 1978)
132. Robert Triffin, *Gold and the Dollar Crisis: Yesterday and Tomorrow*. (Dec. 1978)
133. Herbert G. Grubel, *A Proposal for the Establishment of an International Deposit Insurance Corporation*. (July 1979)
134. Bertil Ohlin, *Some Insufficiencies in the Theories of International Economic Relations*. (Sept. 1979)
135. Frank A. Southard, Jr., *The Evolution of the International Monetary Fund*. (Dec. 1979)
136. Niels Thygesen, *Exchange-Rate Experiences and Policies of Small Countries: Some European Examples in the 1970s*. (Dec. 1979)
137. Robert M. Dunn, Jr., *Exchange Rates, Payments Adjustments, and OPEC: Why Oil Deficits Persist*. (Dec. 1979)
138. Tom de Vries, *On the Meaning and Future of the European Monetary System*. (Sept. 1980)
139. Deepak Lal, *A Liberal International Economic Order: The International Monetary System and Economic Development*. (Oct. 1980)
140. Pieter Korteweg, *Exchange-Rate Policy, Monetary Policy, and Real Exchange-Rate Variability*. (Dec. 1980)
141. Bela Balassa, *The Process of Industrial Development and Alternative Development Strategies*. (Dec. 1980)
142. Benjamin J. Cohen, *The European Monetary System: An Outsider's View*. (June 1981)
143. Marina v. N. Whitman, *International Trade and Investment: Two Perspectives*. (July 1981)
144. Sidney Dell, *On Being Grandmotherly: The Evolution of IMF Conditionality*. (Oct. 1981)
145. Ronald I. McKinnon and Donald J. Mathieson, *How to Manage a Repressed Economy*. (Dec. 1981)

*146. Bahram Nowzad, *The IMF and Its Critics*. (Dec. 1981)

147. Edmar Lisboa Bacha and Carlos F. Díaz Alejandro, *International Financial Intermediation: A Long and Tropical View*. (May 1982)
148. Alan A. Rabin and Leland B. Yeager, *Monetary Approaches to the Balance of Payments and Exchange Rates*. (Nov. 1982)
149. C. Fred Bergsten, Rudiger Dornbusch, Jacob A. Frenkel, Steven W. Kohl-

*Out of print. Available on demand in xerographic paperback or library-bound copies from University Microfilms International, Box 1467, Ann Arbor, Michigan 48106, United States, and 30-32 Mortimer St., London, WIN 7RA, England. Paperback reprints are usually $20. Microfilm of all Essays by year is also available from University Microfilms. Photocopied sheets of out-of-print titles are available on demand from the Section at $6 per Essay and $8 per Study or Special Paper.

hagen, Luigi Spaventa, and Thomas D. Willett, *From Rambouillet to Versailles: A Symposium*. (Dec. 1982)

150. Robert E. Baldwin, *The Inefficacy of Trade Policy*. (Dec. 1982)
151. Jack Guttentag and Richard Herring, *The Lender-of-Last Resort Function in an International Context*. (May 1983)
152. G. K. Helleiner, *The IMF and Africa in the 1980s*. (July 1983)
153. Rachel McCulloch, *Unexpected Real Consequences of Floating Exchange Rates*. (Aug. 1983)
154. Robert M. Dunn, Jr., *The Many Disappointments of Floating Exchange Rates*. (Dec. 1983)
155. Stephen Marris, *Managing the World Economy: Will We Ever Learn?* (Oct. 1984)
156. Sebastian Edwards, *The Order of Liberalization of the External Sector in Developing Countries*. (Dec. 1984)
157. Wilfred J. Ethier and Richard C. Marston, eds., with Kindleberger, Guttentag and Herring, Wallich, Henderson, and Hinshaw, *International Financial Markets and Capital Movements: A Symposium in Honor of Arthur I. Bloomfield*. (Sept. 1985)
158. Charles E. Dumas, *The Effects of Government Deficits: A Comparative Analysis of Crowding Out*. (Oct. 1985)
159. Jeffrey A. Frankel, *Six Possible Meanings of "Overvaluation": The 1981-85 Dollar*. (Dec. 1985)
160. Stanley W. Black, *Learning from Adversity: Policy Responses to Two Oil Shocks*. (Dec. 1985)
161. Alexis Rieffel, *The Role of the Paris Club in Managing Debt Problems*. (Dec. 1985)
162. Stephen E. Haynes, Michael M. Hutchison, and Raymond F. Mikesell, *Japanese Financial Policies and the U.S. Trade Deficit*. (April 1986)
163. Arminio Fraga, *German Reparations and Brazilian Debt: A Comparative Study*. (July 1986)

PRINCETON STUDIES IN INTERNATIONAL FINANCE

44. Clas Wihlborg, *Currency Risks in International Financial Markets*. (Dec. 1978)
45. Ian M. Drummond, *London, Washington, and the Management of the Franc, 1936-39*. (Nov. 1979)
46. Susan Howson, *Sterling's Managed Float: The Operations of the Exchange Equalisation Account, 1932-39*. (Nov. 1980)
47. Jonathan Eaton and Mark Gersovitz, *Poor Country Borrowing in Private Financial Markets and the Repudiation Issue*. (June 1981)
48. Barry J. Eichengreen, *Sterling and the Tariff, 1929-32*. (Sept. 1981)
49. Peter Bernholz, *Flexible Exchange Rates in Historical Perspective*. (July 1982)
50. Victor Argy, *Exchange-Rate Management in Theory and Practice*. (Oct. 1982)
51. Paul Wonnacott, *U.S. Intervention in the Exchange Market for DM, 1977-80*. (Dec. 1982)
52. Irving B. Kravis and Robert E. Lipsey, *Toward an Explanation of National Price Levels*. (Nov. 1983)
53. Avraham Ben-Bassat, *Reserve-Currency Diversification and the Substitution Account*. (March 1984)

*54. Jeffrey Sachs, *Theoretical Issues in International Borrowing*. (July 1984)
55. Marsha R. Shelburn, *Rules for Regulating Intervention under a Managed Float*. (Dec. 1984)
56. Paul De Grauwe, Marc Janssens, and Hilde Leliaert, *Real-Exchange-Rate Variability from 1920 to 1926 and 1973 to 1982*. (Sept. 1985)

SPECIAL PAPERS IN INTERNATIONAL ECONOMICS

8. Jagdish Bhagwati, *The Theory and Practice of Commercial Policy: Departures from Unified Exchange Rates*. (Jan. 1968)
*9. Marina von Neumann Whitman, *Policies for Internal and External Balance*. (Dec. 1970)
10. Richard E. Caves, *International Trade, International Investment, and Imperfect Markets*. (Nov. 1974)
*11. Edward Tower and Thomas D. Willett, *The Theory of Optimum Currency Areas and Exchange-Rate Flexibility*. (May 1976)
*12. Ronald W. Jones, *"Two-ness" in Trade Theory: Costs and Benefits*. (April 1977)
13. Louka T. Katseli-Papaefstratiou, *The Reemergence of the Purchasing Power Parity Doctrine in the 1970s*. (Dec. 1979)
*14. Morris Goldstein, *Have Flexible Exchange Rates Handicapped Macroeconomic Policy?* (June 1980)
15. Gene M. Grossman and J. David Richardson, *Strategic Trade Policy: A Survey of Issues and Early Analysis*. (April 1985)

REPRINTS IN INTERNATIONAL FINANCE

18. Peter B. Kenen, *Floats, Glides and Indicators: A Comparison of Methods for Changing Exchange Rates*. [Reprinted from *Journal of International Economics*, 5 (May 1975).] (June 1975)
19. Polly R. Allen and Peter B. Kenen, *The Balance of Payments, Exchange Rates, and Economic Policy: A Survey and Synthesis of Recent Developments*. [Reprinted from Center of Planning and Economic Research, Occasional Paper 33, Athens, Greece, 1978.] (April 1979)
20. William H. Branson, *Asset Markets and Relative Prices in Exchange Rate Determination*. [Reprinted from *Sozialwissenschaftliche Annalen*, Vol. 1, 1977.] (June 1980)
21. Peter B. Kenen, *The Analytics of a Substitution Account*. [Reprinted from *Banca Nazionale del Lavoro Quarterly Review*, No. 139 (Dec. 1981).] (Dec. 1981)
22. Jorge Braga de Macedo, *Exchange Rate Behavior with Currency Inconvertibility*. [Reprinted from *Journal of International Economics*, 12 (Feb. 1982).] (Sept. 1982)
23. Peter B. Kenen, *Use of the SDR to Supplement or Substitute for Other Means of Finance*. [Reprinted from George M. von Furstenberg, ed., *International Money and Credit: The Policy Roles*, Washington, IMF, 1983, Chap. 7.] (Dec. 1983)
24. Peter B. Kenen, *Forward Rates, Interest Rates, and Expectations under Alternative Exchange Rate Regimes*. [Reprinted from *Economic Record*, 61 (September 1985).] (June 1986)